DA MONEY MANUAL

Financial Freedom for Folks Who Never Got Da Game

KAMARLO SPOONER
"MARLO DA MOTIVATOR"

Copyright © 2025 by Kamarlo Spooner

All rights reserved. No part of this publication may be reproduced, stored in a retrieval system, or transmitted in any form or by any means—electronic, mechanical, photocopying, recording, or otherwise—without the prior written permission of the author, except in the case of brief quotations embodied in critical articles or reviews.

Book Design by Aeyshaa

ISBN: 9781736225189
Library of Congress Control Number: 2025912785

Dedication

To God be the glory.

This book wouldn't exist without His mercy, His correction, and His favor.

So I dedicate it first to the One who saw me through every storm and trusted me with the testimony.

This book is dedicated to the people who were never handed the blueprint.

Even to those of you who were never taught how money works.

To those who didn't have access to wealth-building game but still showed up every day and fought to survive anyway.

It's dedicated to the younger me…

And to every person who had to figure it out the hard way.

And to my wife

You've been with me through every step.

Even when we disagreed, you stood by me, encouraged me, and believed in what we were building.

You took the time out to read every word of every book that I have written, corrected every mistake, and learned this game right alongside me.

This book wouldn't exist without you.

To all of you this book is a piece of my heart, my hustle, and my hope.

Now the tools are in your hands.

Do something with them.

A wise man once said, "Excuses are for people that expect to fail."
~ Mr. Tip "T.I." Harris

So I say to you: no more excuses.

"Because the only thing standing between you and the life you want… is the excuse that you're willing to tell yourself to not go get it.

WINNERS WIN AND LOSERS.
WELL, THEY JUST LOSE!

TABLE OF CONTENTS

Da 100,000,000 Million Dollar Question!!! 6

Introduction 8

Chapter 1:
Da Money Mindset Shift 11

Chapter 2:
Da Budget Breakdown 19

Chapter 3:
Da Credit Comeback 27

Chapter 4:
Da Saving Strategy 36

Chapter 5:
Da Debt Detox 43

Chapter 6:
Da Side Hustle's Hustle 49

Chapter 7:
Da Investment Intro 57

Chapter 8:
Da Legacy Blueprint 65

Bonus Chapters:
Chapter 1:
Da Most Common Money Mistakes
(And How To Avoid 'Em) 72

Chapter 2:
Real-Life Lessons From A Ziplock Bank With Family 78

Chapter 3:
Tryna Look Rich Vs. Gettin' Rich : Da Broke Flex Trap 83

Chapter 4:
Real Talk About Unions That Pay 90

DA 100,000,000 MILLION DOLLAR QUESTION!!!

> *"You're in the real estate game. The question is: What side are you on?"*
> ~ *Marlo Da Motivator*

I once gave a lecture to a room of over 100 people.

I asked, **"How many of y'all are in the real estate game?"**

Not a single hand went up.

Then I asked, "How many of you pay rent to a landlord every month?"

Every hand in the room shot up.

So, I looked them straight into their eyes and gave them the truth:

You are in the real estate game, you're just on the wrong side of it.

Because every time you pay rent, your landlord is probably keeping some for their own bills and sending the rest to the bank to pay down their mortgage.

One day, they'll own that house that you currently live in free and clear… How? By using your hard-earned money.

And then I told them:

You guys are some very nice people. Why don't you give yourself a round of applause. And I started clapping. No one else clapped, some started laughing while others sat there and were stunned.

I'm now telling you. Yes, that's right, You, the person that is reading this book. You're helping someone else build generational wealth.

But now it's time to flip that playa.

Da Money Manual: Financial Freedom for Folks Who Never Got Da Game

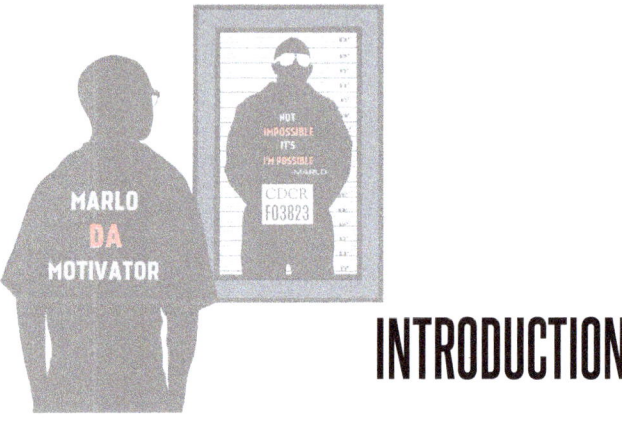

INTRODUCTION

Da Day I Came Home With $200 and a Vision

I had been incarcerated for 3 years, 3 months, 2 weeks, and 3 days, and I was finally being released.

By the time I walked out of that prison, here's what I had to my name:

- A credit score of 444
- No car, it had been repo'd
- No house
- No valid driver's license
- $200 in my pocket (that the system gave me)
- Two misdemeanors, two felonies and a strike on my record
- On parole and on probation at the same time

Most people would've said I didn't have a chance.

But I had something that didn't show up on paper baby:

Faith. Hunger. And a vision that wouldn't quit.

My wife was waiting for me in the car in the prison parking lot. We went straight to Denny's for breakfast. I needed some food that was better than that prison food. After we paid, I had about $163 left.

We picked up our two daughters and checked into a hotel for the night.

We didn't even have a place to stay, my wife had been crashing at a friend's.

Even the car she picked me up in was at risk, she was behind on the notes.

We were praying they wouldn't find it and repo it while we were out grabbing breakfast.

That's how tight things were.

A few days later, I checked in with my parole officer.

After hearing everything I had going on, he looked at me and said:

"You should go jump off a bridge. Your life is over." Kill yourself.

Can you believe that?

But I once heard a wise man named Les Brown say:

"Don't let someone's opinion of you become your reality."

And you know what??? I didn't. Let me stop here long enough to tell you that within 2 years I was earning just as much as he (My Probation Officer) was.

Today, as I sit here writing this manual...

- We own three 4-bedroom, 2-bathroom homes and two 2-bedroom 1-bedroom rental units
- We run a successful trucking company
- I've written and published six books

- My credit score is 839
- My driver's license is valid and clean
- My misdemeanors have been expunged
- And I received a Certificate of Rehabilitation and Pardon from the Superior Court of Alameda County
- I have earned not 1, but 5 Associate Degrees, a Bachelor Degree, and I am enrolled in a Graduate Program working towards my Master's in Public Administration degree.

This ain't bragging. This is proof.

It's proof that even if you've made mistakes…

Even if they tried to count you out…

Even if they told you that you should go jump off of a bridge.

Even if you're coming home with nothing but $200 and a vision, you can make it.

This book is Da Money Manual: Financial Freedom for Folks Who Never Got Da Game.

I'm about to give you the playbook I never had but always needed.

Let's get to it.

CHAPTER 1:
DA MONEY MINDSET SHIFT

"You can't build wealth with a broke mentality."
~ Marlo Da Motivator

Before you can fix your wallet, you gotta fix your way of thinking.

See, nobody ever gave us da game when it came to money. In school, we were taught how to be employees. We were taught to be at school (and eventually work) by 8 a.m.

We learned how to take a 15-minute break aka "recess" then get back to work. Then came lunch break. Sound familiar?

We were pushed to memorize things like the periodic table and powers and exponents. I'm not saying those things aren't useful, but they're not useful for everybody.

Pay attention to this question. Do you know what they didn't teach? The Real-Life Stuff. I am not talking about the one semester of economics that they spoon feed you. I am talking about the things that create real generational wealth.

- How to manage a savings account.

- How to build wealth using money market accounts or stocks.

- How to buy property using other people's money, and let tenants pay off the loan.

- How to refinance a house, pull cash out, and buy another one.

- How to get rich and be a boss, a CEO, a tycoon!

They trained us to follow the system. But never how to own anything in it.

On the streets we were taught survival, not strategy. Fast cash, not long-term plans. So, we picked up habits from the block, the struggle, or our own people, folks who were doing the best they could, but didn't know better either.

We laughed at credit. Spent the rent money. Borrowed cashed to flex. And then blamed ourselves for being "bad with money," when the truth is, we were just uninformed, not unworthy.

This chapter ain't about math. It's about mindset. Because until you shift how you see money; you'll always stay stuck in the same cycle.

Your First Shift:

From: "I'll always be broke"

To: "I'm learning how to manage and multiply money."

The way you talk to yourself about money matters. Speak like you're building something, even if you're just getting started.

Real Story: Writing Myself Out the Hole

Before I came home from prison, I realized that if I wanted to change my life, I had to start with my mindset.

So, I began reading positive books. I started speaking life over my situation. I even wrote letters to my future self while I was still locked up.

I mailed those letters home to our P.O. box because we didn't even have a house or apartment of our own at the time.

I told my wife not to open them. Those letters were for me to read once I got out.

In those letters, I told myself everything I hated about being in jail and prison.

I wrote out my vision. I listed all the ways I could save money a little at a time.

Because when you're in one of the hardest seasons of your life especially when you're by yourself, if you dig deep enough, you'll come up with some powerful ideas.

But you gotta be focused.

I watched men in prison get hundreds of dollars from their families every month.

And every time that money hit their books, they spent every dime expeditiously.

Not just on extra food, chips, cookies, donuts, candy, sodas, and juices, but on fancy soaps, name-brand toothpaste, and things they didn't even need.

They gambled over cards, bet on basketball and football games, and blew money with no regard for the people who were sacrificing to send it to them.

I didn't do that.

I asked my wife to send me just $40 a month. That was it. Some months I asked my sisters to send the $40 so that one person wouldn't feel all of the pressure of helping me. That meant that one person gave me help every 3 or 4 months. It didn't hurt them so bad to do that.

I bought only what I needed and enough Top Ramen to stretch for the month.

This may sound funny, but I even broke a few of the packs of noodles in half sometimes, half for the day, half for the night.

I used the free soap and the free toothpaste that the prison provided.

I ate the three meals the prison served, like everybody else should have been doing.

Why?

Because I wasn't thinking about just surviving, I was thinking more about Thriving!

I was thinking about stacking. About credit. About freedom even before I got there physically, I was there mentally and so should you be.

You want to shift your money situation?

You've got to be willing to make adjustments.

You've got to be willing to sacrifice.

That's the mindset that leads to real change.

Real Talk Journal Prompt:

- What were you taught (directly or indirectly) about money growing up?

- What limiting beliefs do you carry today?

- When did you first realize money was more emotional than logical?

Chapter 1:

Da Money Mindset Shift

Your Mindset Moves

Write out the beliefs you're shifting, the broke talk you're replacing, and how you're starting to think like wealth is possible for you.

_____

_____

_____

_____

_____

_____

_____

_____

_____

_____

_____

_____

CHAPTER 2:
DA BUDGET BREAKDOWN

"Money disappears faster when you don't tell it where to go."
~ Marlo Da Motivator

Real Talk First:

Let's be real, most people weren't taught how to budget.

We were told, *"Don't spend more than you make,"* but nobody showed us how to do that when rent, food, gas, and life are all punching your pockets at once.

Budgeting ain't about being broke it's about being in control.

It doesn't matter if you make $500 a week or $5,000, if you don't have a plan, your money will be gone before you realize it.

What Is a Budget (For Real)?

A budget is simply telling your money what to do and where to go, instead of wondering what it did and where it went. Ya Feel Me!

It's not punishment. It's power.

It's your playbook. It's how you make sure your goals eat before your cravings do.

Some of you need to starve our wants, and feed yall goals.

Quick Exercise:

Before we break this down, answer this honestly:

- When's the last time you tracked every dollar you spent in a week?

- How often do you feel like you should have more money than what's actually in your account?

- What's one expense you know you could cut back on (even a little)?

The 3-Bucket Budget (Simple Gameplan)

1. MUST HAVES (50%)

Rent, food, transportation, utilities. The stuff that keeps your life running.

2. FUTURE MONEY (30%)

Savings, paying down debt, building your credit. This is how you level up.

3. FUN + FLEX (20%)

Clothes, streaming, going out, gifts. Fun is allowed, but only after your priorities are paid.

"If you ain't budgeting, you're just freelancing with your finances." And to be honest, that's a sucka move.
~ Marlo Da Motivator

I've seen what it looks like when someone wants to change… but ain't ready yet.

My mom used to smoke cigarettes. And for years, she'd tell me, "I'm gonna quit, baby."

She said it so much that after a while, I stopped paying attention, because every time I saw her, she still had a cigarette in her hand.

Then one day, she told me she was trying something new, she had switched to nicotine gum. I thought, Okay, maybe she's serious now.

But I still saw her smoking.

Then came the patch. "This is supposed to help," she said.

But it got to a point where I saw her wearing the patch, chewing the gum, and still lighting up a cigarette, all at the same time.

Then she got the news. Cancer.

And do you know what she did?

She quit that same day. Cold turkey. Never picked one up again.

That's when it hit me:

She kept saying she wanted to change, but it wasn't until she had to change that she finally did.

So, I'm asking you: Have you reached your "had to" moment?

Have you reached that moment where it's not just "I want to," but **"I got to"**?

Because when you hit that point, that breaking point, the change is real.

And if you can't do it for yourself… do it for your kids. Do it for your mother. Your father.

Do it for something bigger than you.

Money Move: Finding Hidden Money in Our Budget

When we finally found our first super small ADU apartment to live in: it was a small unit behind the owner's house. I realized something:

We weren't making it through the month financially. We were taking out small pay day advances from Wells Fargo and then they (Wells Fargo) would pull it out of my direct deposit pay checks each week before my check cleared to me.

By this time, I had started working. So, I sat down and looked at where all our money was going.

And what I found shocked me.

We were paying for a high cable package, and we didn't even watch most of the channels!

So I picked up the phone, called the cable company, and told them I was canceling.

I told them another provider was offering a better deal, and that we didn't need all those channels anyway.

They ended up giving me a $35 monthly credit that lasted for a year (which every year I kept calling back to them for them to renew it and they did) and they let me downgrade our plan.

That alone saved us almost $55 per month.

Then I called our cell phone provider and did the same thing, cut the plan and cut the cost.

It might not sound like a lot to some people, but we were able to stop getting those pay day advances because of the moves and over time, we were able to start saving: it adds up big mane.

Take Action:

Write down your real monthly income and divide it into the 3 buckets. Be honest.

Monthly Take-Home (after taxes): $_____

- Must Haves (50%): $_____

- Future Money (30%): $_____

- Fun + Flex (20%): $_____

Chapter 2: Da Budget Breakdown

Your Budget Blueprint

Track what your money's doing, plan your next steps, and get real about how you're gonna tell every dollar where to go.

_____

_____

_____

_____

_____

_____

_____

_____

_____

_____

_____

_____

Da Budget Breakdown

CHAPTER 3:
DA CREDIT COMEBACK

> *"Your credit report don't care about your excuses it only sees your behaviors."*
> *~ Marlo Da Motivator*

Real Talk First

I came home from prison with a credit score of 444. That's not just bad credit, that's actually being buried.

No one taught us how credit works.

We just heard, "Don't mess it up."

But credit ain't a trap it's a tool. And when you understand the game, you can flip it in your favor.

This chapter is for everyone who's ever felt like their score was too far gone to fix.

I'm here to tell you: you can bounce back. I did.

What Is Credit (Really)?

Credit is your reputation with money.

It's how banks, landlords, businesses, and even some jobs decide if they can trust you to hire you and or to allow you to borrow some bread and pay them back.

Your credit score is built from 5 things:

1. **Payment History (35%)** – Do you pay your bills on time?
2. **Credit Usage (30%)** – How much of your available credit are you using?
3. **Credit Age (15%)** – How long have your accounts been open?
4. **Mix of Credit (10%)** – Do you have a mix (cards, loans, etc.)?
5. **Inquiries (10%)** – How often are you applying for credit?

Quick Credit Check-In

- Do you know your credit score?
- When's the last time you checked it?
- Do you know what's hurting your score the most right now?
- What's one positive move you've made (or can make) this month?

Simple Steps to Start Rebuilding

- Pull your credit reports (free at annualcreditreport.com)
- Dispute errors even small ones can hurt you
- Pay your bills on time, even if it's just the minimum
- Get a secured credit card (use it for small purchases, pay it off monthly)

- Keep your usage under 30% don't max out your cards

What's a Secured Credit Card?

A secured credit card is a special kind of credit card for people who are trying to build or fix their credit.

Here's how it works:

- You put down a cash deposit (like $200)
- That deposit becomes your credit limit
- You use the card and pay it off on time
- The bank reports your payments to the credit bureaus

After a few months of responsible use, your score starts to go up, and many times, they'll offer you a regular unsecured card later on.

Think of it like training wheels for your credit. You know, basically you are frontin' yourself some cash on a credit card.

> *"Credit ain't about being rich it's about being responsible and trustworthy."*
> **~ Marlo Da Motivator**

Money Move: Negotiating My Way Out of Debt

I remember pulling my credit report for the first time after getting out, and what I saw hit me hard.

There was the car that got repoed while I was locked up...

Two credit cards I couldn't pay during my sentence...

The damage was clear:

One account "da car" said I still owed $7,988.

That debt was already about 4 years old, since I was inside the whole time.

So I did something most people don't think to do I called them.

I got the number straight off the credit report, picked up the phone, and said:

"Look, here's my story. I've been down. I've been locked up. But I'm trying to do things right."

I told them I had $979, and I'd give it to them if they marked it as "paid in full" on my credit report.

They said no at first.

So, I told them the truth:

"Then you won't get anything. I'll just wait for it to fall off in a couple years." Listen: Here is some game for yall. After 7 years, negative credit falls off or should I say it stop having a negative effect on your credit. All I had to do was to wait a few more years.

They paused… then they agreed. They realized that some money is better than no money. Ya feel me.

That account got marked as paid in full. That means that any company that pulls my credit now looks at me as responsible, at least on that particular account.

Then I called the two credit card companies.

I owed over $1,500 on each.

I offered $255 to one, and $335 to the other.

They both accepted. I told them to put it in writing and once I received the email that they were going to remove the negative information from my credit report, I cashed them out.. Always get it in writing before paying these cats.

And not only did they mark the accounts settled,

they removed them completely from my credit report as they stated.

After those moves?

My score jumped to around 649.

That was the beginning of my credit comeback.

Strategy: Don't Try to Fix Everything

Let me say this clearly:

You don't have to fix every old thing on your credit report.

If something is close to falling off like 6 or 7 years old and it's not reporting monthly?

Let it fall off. Don't wake it up.

When you call or make a payment, you might reset the clock on that debt. That means that they can start your 7-year window over again. Be smart!!

So unless it's blocking you from moving forward (like buying a house), it's sometimes smarter to just let it fade away like a Michal Jordan, Kobe Byrant or should I say a Anthoy Edward's jump shot.

Credit isn't about fixing everything.

It's about moving strategically.

That's what I did and today, I'm sitting on an 839 score.

Credit Myths That Keep People Stuck

❌ **Myth:** You have to pay every single debt to fix your credit.

✅ **Truth:** Some debts are better left alone if they're old and inactive.

❌ **Myth:** Paying off collections makes them disappear.

✅ **Truth:** Not unless they agree to remove it always ask first and get it in writing before paying.

❌ **Myth:** Checking your credit score hurts it.

✅ **Truth:** Only hard inquiries hurt your score. Pulling your own report is safe and has no impact on your score.

❌ **Myth:** You need to carry a balance to build credit.

✅ **Truth:** You build credit by paying on time. Carrying a balance only means paying interest.

Take Action

This month, choose one thing to do:

- Set up auto-pay on one bill
- Pull and review your credit reports
- Open a secured credit card and use it wisely
- Write a plan to pay off one small debt

Chapter 3: Da Credit Comeback

✎ Your Credit Comeback Plan

Note what you learned about credit, what you need to fix, and your first steps toward building that 700+ score.

CHAPTER 4:
DA SAVING STRATEGY

"If you can't save while you're broke, you won't save when you're rich."
~ Marlo Da Motivator

Real Talk First

Most people think they don't have a saving problem. They think they just don't have enough money.

But saving isn't about how much you make. It's about how you move with what you have.

When I came home, I was starting from scratch. But I realized fast that if I waited until everything was perfect, I'd never start.

Saving is more than a financial move. It's a mindset. It's you telling your future, "I got cha."

Why Most People Don't Save

- They think they don't make enough
- They spend without tracking

- They treat savings like "extra" instead of making it a priority
- They don't have a plan, just vibes

Building a Saving System That Works

Let's keep it simple. Break your savings into three categories:

1. **Emergency Fund** – Life is going to life. A flat tire, medical bill, or job loss shouldn't take you out
1. **Short-Term Goals** – Birthdays, holidays, school clothes, back-to-school expenses
1. **Big Moves Fund** – Business ideas, a down payment, or that one thing that could change your life. Start small, but start

How Much Should You Save?

- Aim to save 5 to 10 percent of whatever you bring in
- If that's too much, start with just five dollars a week
- Consistency matters more than amount
- Set up auto-transfer if you can
- Don't touch your savings. That's not your backup checking account

Money Move: From Takeout to Stackin'

When we were first getting back on our feet, I looked at our money and realized something else.

We were spending way too much eating out. Three to four times a week. It didn't seem like much at first, but those meals were draining us.

So, we sat down and tracked where our money was going.

We made a choice to start cooking more and cut back on the extras.

That decision alone helped us save a couple hundred dollars a month.

Once we saw the difference, we looked at everything else.

Cable? Switched to a smaller plan

Cell phones? Called and negotiated a cheaper rate

Monthly apps and subscriptions? Cut them off

It all added up. It was slow, but it stacked.

Saving isn't about missing out.

It's about being serious enough to sacrifice now so you can breathe later.

Let's Get Practical

Start with a Goal: $500 Hustle Fund → $1,000 Emergency Fund

Don't get overwhelmed thinking you need ten grand to start saving.

Start by stacking $500, your hustle fund.

That's money for unexpected bills, small investments, or moments where you need to move fast.

Once you hit that, aim for $1,000. That becomes your emergency cushion.

Small steps turn into real protection.

Bank Account vs. Mattress Money

Keeping cash in a drawer or under the bed feels safe, but it can hold you back.

If you ever want to buy a house, a car, or anything with a loan, lenders will want to see proof of where your money came from.

You can't just show up with 10 racks in cash and expect them to take it. They want seasoned funds, money they can see moving through your account over time. For all they know, that is dope money.

So, putting your money in a bank account isn't just smart.

It's necessary if you're planning for something bigger.

Saving isn't about what you can't have, it's about what you're willing to wait for.
~ Marlo Da Motivator

Take Action

Pick one of these saving strategies and commit to it this month:

- The Five Dollar Envelope Challenge: Every time you get a five, stash it

- Thirty Day No-Spend Challenge: No extras, no fast food, no impulse buys. Track how much you save

- Auto-Save Rule: Automatically move money to savings each payday

- Round-Up App: Some apps round every purchase up and save the spare change. Let tech help you save without thinking about it

Chapter 4: Da Saving Strategy

💰 *Your Stacking Strategy*

Jot down what you're saving for, how much you can start with, and where you can cut to stack more

_____

_____

_____

_____

_____

_____

_____

_____

_____

_____

_____

_____

_____

Da Saving Strategy

CHAPTER 5:
DA DEBT DETOX

"Debt kept calling me by name, but I stopped answering."
~ Marlo Da Motivator

Real Talk First

Debt can feel like quicksand. One minute you're managing things, the next you're drowning in payments, fees, and stress.

Some of us were raised in homes where borrowing was survival.

Credit cards covered groceries. Payday loans filled the gap. Store cards made Christmas happen.

And before we knew it, debt became normal, and so did the pressure that came with it.

But here's the truth:

You don't owe anybody your peace.

And you don't have to live in debt for the rest of your life.

The Most Common Types of Debt

- Credit cards
- Auto loans
- Personal loans
- Student loans
- Medical bills
- Old utility or phone bills

All debt is not created equal, but all debt needs a plan.

Step One: Know What You Owe

You can't fight what you won't face.

Write down every single debt, no matter how old or how small.

Include:

- Who you owe
- The balance
- The interest rate
- The minimum payment
- Whether it's current or in collections

This step alone can feel heavy, but once it's on paper, you're in control.

Step Two: Pick a Payoff Strategy

The Avalanche Method

Pay off the debt with the highest interest first.

You'll save more money in the long run.

The Snowball Method

Pay off the smallest balance first to get quick wins and build momentum.

Pick one that fits your mindset and your money. The key is staying consistent.

Step Three: Start Making Real Moves

- Stop creating new debt
- Call creditors and negotiate lower payments or settlements
- If a debt is in collections, offer a lump sum and ask them to mark it paid in full
- Use your budget and saving habits to free up money for extra payments

Take Action

- List every debt today, all of it
- Choose your payoff strategy
- Make your first extra payment this month, even if it's just ten dollars
- Contact one creditor and try to negotiate

Chapter 5: Da Debt Detox

 *Your Debt Detox Plan*

List the debts you're tackling, the method you're choosing, and what "freedom from debt" will mean for your life

CHAPTER 6:
DA SIDE HUSTLE'S HUSTLE

"If the streets taught you how to flip something, then life can teach you how to flip things as well, just legally."
~ Marlo Da Motivator

Real Talk First

Sometimes the job you got just ain't enough.

Bills stack up. Groceries cost more. And trying to save or pay off debt feels impossible when the math ain't mathing.

That's where the hustle comes in.

I'm not talking about scams, shortcuts, or anything illegal. I'm talking about legal money moves that help you earn more using what you already know, love, or have access to.

If you've ever sold candy in school, flipped sneakers, detailed cars, cut hair, made music, helped people move, or figured out how to stretch a dollar, you already got what it takes.

You just need to flip that energy the right way.

Side Hustles vs. Scams

Let's be clear. A side hustle builds you up. A scam breaks you down. Maybe even get you locked up!

A hustle creates skills, relationships, and income you can grow.

A scam might bring fast cash, but it comes with risk, fear, and usually ends with regret.

Ask yourself:

- Is this legal?
- Does it have long-term potential?
- Would I want my kids or my mother doing this?

If the answer is no to any of them questions, it's not a hustle. It's a setup 4 lock up.

What You Can Do With What You Already Know

Your skills are valuable. The question is, are you using them?

Start by asking:

- What do people already come to me for?
- What do I enjoy doing that solves problems for others?
- What can I do with what's already in my hands?

Examples:

- Good with kids? Babysitting or tutoring
- Know how to braid, cut, or twist hair? Mobile barber or stylist
- Great with cars? Mobile detailing

- Talkative? Start a podcast, YouTube channel, or host events
- Organized? Help people move, declutter, or clean
- Not scared of dirt! Taking old people or even lazy people trash cans out to the curbside on trash collection day and returning them to the back yard after the garbage truck comes to dump them. Here me out: My two sons did this a few years ago when they were 10 and 11 years old. They made extra money. You will be surprised how many people are tired of pulling them dirty, stinky cans in and out of their backyards. They will pay you mane.

Here your guy out! You don't need a big investment. You just need the courage to start small.

Making Legal Money Move Like Street Money Used To

You ever flipped something on the street and made it multiply?

Same mindset, just new product, new process, new purpose.

Think about it:

- You used to hustle to survive. Now hustle to build.
- You used to work for fast money. Now work for freedom money.
- You used to hide what you did. Now build something you can pass down and be proud of.

You don't need to change your grind. Just change your lane.

Money Move: Barbershop Clippers

Back when I first came home, I realized we didn't have a lot of money to work with.

I wanted to look good, stay clean, and feel confident, but I couldn't justify spending thirty to fifty dollars every week on a haircut.

So, I made an executive decision. That is what Bosses, CEO's, Presidents, Leaders, Tycoons do! We make real decisions.

I took a little money and bought a pair of clippers.

They weren't fancy, but they worked.

I taught myself how to cut my own hair. I practiced. I got better. And when I messed up cutting my hair, I didn't give a care. It would grow back. And listen, I've been cutting my own hair since June of 2008.

I don't even have to give some sucka (the barber) a tip anymore. I just give myself the tip by putting that dough away. Straight up!

Now let's do some quick math.

If a haircut cost thirty to fifty dollars per week and there are 52 weeks in each year, and I have been cutting my own hair for over a decade. In fact, it's been 17 years to be exact.

That's thousands of dollars I saved just by learning a new skill and being consistent. Right from the comfort of my house I'm saving dough.

That's what a hustle is.

Not always something flashy, but something that works.

Something that saves you money, builds confidence, and creates opportunity.

You don't always need more money.

Sometimes, you just need more discipline, creativity, and courage to try something new.

Take Action

Pick one idea and make a move:

- Write down five hustle ideas based on what you already know

- Ask three people what they think you're good at

- Sell one thing you no longer use and save the profit

- Post your service or product to your community online or in-person

Chapter 6: Da Side Hustle's Hustle

 *Your Hustle Ideas & Game Plan*

Write down your side hustle ideas, skills you can monetize, and the moves you'll make to earn outside your 9–5.

_____

_____

_____

_____

_____

_____

_____

_____

_____

_____

_____

_____

_____

_____

CHAPTER 7:
DA INVESTMENT INTRO

"Money sitting still ain't money building wealth."
~ *Marlo Da Motivator*

Real Talk First

Most of us were raised to work for money, not to make money work for us.

We were told to get a job, get a check, and just try to make it stretch.

But nobody pulled us aside and said, "Hey, your money can actually grow while you sleep."

That's what investing is about.

Not chasing fast money but planting seeds that build real wealth over time.

You don't need to be rich to start investing. You just need to get in da game.

What Investing Really Means

Investing just means putting your money somewhere it can grow.

That's it. It's not a mystery, it's a move.

It's different from saving.

Saving protects your money.

Investing multiplies it.

The Three Most Common Ways to Start

1. Stocks

Buying a small piece of a company. You make money when the value goes up or when they pay you dividends.

2. Real Estate

Owning property that brings in income (rent) or builds value (equity) over time.

3. Business

Starting your own business or investing in someone else's. This one comes with risk but also reward when done right.

What to Know Before You Start

- Only invest money you can afford to leave alone for a while
- Don't invest just because someone hyped it up online
- Study before you jump
- Start small. Consistency wins
- You don't have to be perfect. You just have to be willing to learn

Bonus Move: Stack It First in a High-Yield Savings Account

Not ready to invest just yet? That's okay.

Start by putting your money in a high-yield savings account instead of a regular one.

It earns more interest, keeps your cash safe, and gives you a place to build your investment fund while you're learning the game.

It's not a wealth builder, but it's a smart, steady first step.

Some Real-World Entry Points

- Use an app like Robinhood or Fidelity to start with as little as $5
- Buy shares in companies you already believe in
- Consider buying a small piece of land or looking into tax lien auctions
- If you have a side hustle, reinvest your profits into tools, marketing, or training
- Look into vending machines, car rentals, or storage units, small businesses that build passive income

Money Move: From a Stolen Car to Real Estate Wins

My wife and I bought our first home with money from our tax return and an insurance payout from a car that got stolen.

Most people would've rushed to buy another car.

But not me.

I took that money, kept it in the bank, and went down to the flea market near the Oakland Coliseum.

I bought myself a used 10-speed bicycle for 27 bucks.

Every morning, rain or shine, I got up at 5:30 a.m. and rode that bike from my house to the Coliseum BART station.

Then I'd take the train into San Francisco, hop off, and ride another 22 minutes to my job.

And I did that same ride all the way back home every night.

While I was stacking, my wife and I started looking at houses. After a few months, we found one we could afford.

We used the money we saved as our down payment.

We lived in that first house for three years.

Then we sold it and used the profit to move into a better neighborhood.

After a few more years, we refinanced and bought our second home and turned that one into a rental.

Later, we used our credit and equity to purchase two more rental units.

What started with a bike, a tax return, and some discipline became a real estate portfolio that's now bringing in passive income and generational wealth for our family. All while we sleep at night and do other thangs in the day!!!

That's what investing looks like when you stop trying to look rich and start thinking long-term.

Take Action

- Pick one area: stocks, real estate, or business
- Read one article or watch one video about how it works

- Set aside a small amount ($10–$25) as your "starter investment" fund

- Ask someone you trust what their first investment looked like

- Start investing in yourself, your education, your mindset, your vision

Chapter 7: Da Investment Intro

Your Investment Game Plan

Track what you wanna invest in, what you still need to learn, and how you're gonna make your money work for you.

_____

_____

_____

_____

_____

_____

_____

_____

_____

_____

_____

_____

_____

_____

Da Investment Intro

CHAPTER 8:
DA LEGACY BLUEPRINT

"The goal ain't just to get money. It's to leave something behind that still speaks after you're gone."
~ Marlo Da Motivator

Real Talk First

Getting money is one thing.

Keeping it is another.

But building something that lives beyond you? That's legacy.

Legacy ain't just for rich people. It's for real people.

The ones who broke cycles. The ones who learned the hard way. The ones who didn't give up.

If you've ever said, "I want my kids to have it better than I had" this chapter is for you.

What Legacy Really Means

Legacy is what people remember about how you lived, what you built, and who you helped.

It's not just money in a will. It's:

- The values you teach
- The businesses you build
- The property you pass down
- The blueprint you leave behind for others to follow

Why Most People Never Build One

- They think they need to be rich
- They stay stuck in survival mode
- They don't realize their story *is* the blueprint
- They don't write anything down
- They don't teach what they learned

You don't need to have millions to leave something meaningful.

You just need to be intentional.

Building Your Legacy (One Step at a Time)

1. **Get Your Paperwork Right**
   - ◊ Create a will
   - ◊ Name a beneficiary on your accounts
   - ◊ Set up life insurance, even a basic policy
   - ◊ Write down your wishes for your kids or your property
2. **Tell Your Story**
   - ◊ Share how you made it

- Teach your family how money works
- Don't just leave things, leave wisdom

3. Own Something

- It can be a house, a business, or even a piece of land
- Ownership is how you break the "start over" cycle
- If you can't buy big, start small. Stack and flip

4. Bless Others While You're Here

- Mentor someone
- Speak life into the next generation
- Give your people the game while you're still alive

Money Move: The Blueprint I'm Leaving Behind

I don't plan to leave this earth without leaving something behind.

At the very least, I plan to leave each of my children their own house, and a lot of land they can split. Listen, owning land, is actually owning a piece of the earth.

That's the bare minimum.

But I'm also leaving them something just as valuable, books.

Books written by their father.

Books they might not even read right now, but when the time is right, they'll open them.

Right after they open the Bible to get wisdom, they'll be opening the books written by me and they'll be able to hear my voice on every page.

Lessons. Struggles. Wisdom. Truth. Straight from me, Straight from daddy.

I believe in that old seat belt car commercial slogan:

"You can learn a lot from a dummy."

Even if I made mistakes, I turned them into manuals.

And I'm not stopping there.

There won't be a sign at my grave that reads "Here Lies a Bum."

Not a chance.

I plan to show my kids how to win.

I want them to pick up where I left off and take it even higher.

They should never believe that weak phrase that say "the sky is the limit."

Because I'm teaching them what Mr. Master P once said, **"Ain't No Limit."**

Take Action

- Write down your legacy goals, what do you want to leave behind?

- Make a list of people you want to bless or teach while you're still here

- Record a voice memo or video telling your story

- Start having money talks with your kids, grandkids, or younger siblings

- Look into a will, life insurance, or how to transfer what you own

Chapter 8: Da Legacy Blueprint

Your Legacy Notes

Who are you doing this for? Write your plan to protect your people, teach the next gen, and leave something that lasts.

BONUS CHAPTERS:
CHAPTER 1:
DA MOST COMMON MONEY MISTAKES (AND HOW TO AVOID 'EM)

"Money mistakes aren't the end. The only real end is when you stop trying, or when you die. Bounce back and build better."
~ Kamarlo "Marlo Da Motivator" Spooner

Intro:

Let's be real, most of us didn't get taught how money works. We learned through pain, pressure, and overdraft fees. This chapter isn't about making you feel bad. It's about showing you the traps, so you don't fall in them.

Because once you know better, you can do better.

1. Spending More Than You Make

- Living paycheck to paycheck is normalized, but it keeps you stuck.

- Overspending often comes from emotional spending or trying to keep up appearances.

- **The fix:** Budget. Track. Adjust. Live below your means now so you can live how you want later.

2. Ignoring Your Credit

- Bad credit can cost you thousands in interest or deny you housing and job opportunities.

- Many ignore it out of fear, but that only makes it worse.

- **The fix:** Pull your report. Face it. Fix it. (See Chapter 3.)

3. Not Saving for Emergencies

- One flat tire shouldn't destroy your whole life.

- Emergencies are guaranteed, prepare for them like you know they're coming.

- **The fix:** Start small. Even $10/week adds up. Hustle up your first $500.

4. Using Debt as a Lifestyle

- Credit cards aren't free money. Loans aren't blessings if they keep you broke.

- **The fix:** Cut back. Pay off what you owe. Build wealth with what you keep, not what you borrow.

5. Thinking a Degree Is the Only Path to Success

- College ain't the only way, and it ain't cheap. Many people rack up debt for degrees they don't use.

- **The fix:** Know your options. There are trade jobs and certifications that pay **very well** without college debt.

🔧 Real Talk: Don't Sleep on These Trade Jobs

If you're ready to level up but college isn't your lane, look at these trades. They're high paying, in demand, and full of opportunity:

Trade Job	Average Salary	Notes
Electrician	$66,000–$100,000+	Start with an apprenticeship
Plumber	$65,000–$100,000+	Strong demand, especially in cities
HVAC Technician	$60,000–$95,000+	Heating/cooling systems expert
Commercial Driver (CDL)	$70,000–$100,000+	Freight, hazmat, or long-haul = more dough
Welder	$65,000–$100,000+	Skilled welders are in high demand
Elevator Installer/Repair	$90,000–$130,000+	One of the highest-paid trades
Wind Turbine Tech	$75,000–$95,000+	Growing field. Clean energy.
Dental Hygienist	$85,000–$100,000+	2-year degree. Flexible schedule.
Auto Technician	$65,000–$90,000+	Especially high if you specialize
IT Support Specialist	$65,000–$95,000+	Certs like CompTIA A+ can open doors fast

The takeaway: There are legal, legit, high-paying ways to build your bag, even without a degree. Find what fits **you**.

Final Word:

Money mistakes don't mean you failed. They mean you learned. Now flip the lesson into a blessing.

You've got the blueprint now.

Da Most Common Money Mistakes (And How to Avoid 'Em)

CHAPTER 2:
REAL-LIFE LESSONS FROM A ZIPLOCK BANK WITH FAMILY

"Real wealth starts with the small lessons at home."
~ Kamarlo "Marlo Da Motivator" Spooner

Real Talk First

Money lessons don't have to come from Wall Street, they can come from your own kitchen table.

I learned that some of the most powerful lessons we teach our kids don't require fancy charts or accounts, just consistency, a little creativity, and some Ziplock bags.

This chapter isn't about theories. It's about what I do in real life, with my real kids, to make money make sense early.

The Story

One of the things I do with my children is this: when they earn allowance for hard work and chores, they like to spend it on buying internal items in PlayStation games like Fortnite. Instead of letting them swipe their own cash away on something digital and fleeting, I use my credit card to make the purchase, and they hand me their money in cash.

But here's the twist, I don't spend the money they give me. I stash it away in plastic Ziplock bags labeled with each of their names and hide them. At the end of the year, I pull them out.

When my kids see those bags, their eyes get big. Then I show them exactly how much money they handed over throughout the year, and how much they spent on video games they no longer play. The realization hits. They're surprised, sometimes even shocked, by how much money went to things they no longer care about.

The next year, they always try to spend less. If they succeed, I show them how much they saved, and then I add interest, just like a real bank would. But we take it a step further. I ask them if they want to invest their money. I give them a couple of ideas, and we even do joint investments, like a family partnership.

I tell them we're investing in the "Marlo Da Motivator Savings Bond." If they say yes, I make it happen. At the end of the quarter or year, I pay them their return on investment.

They love seeing how much more their money grows when they save or invest instead of spending. And best of all, they're learning the value of money, how it works, and how to make it work for them.

Money Move: Teaching Your Kids the Real Value of a Dollar

Instead of letting my kids waste their allowance, I turned it into a hidden savings account and a lesson in wealth. At the end of the year, we looked at what they spent, what they saved, and how money could grow. That's not just parenting. That's building generational money habits.

Real Talk Reflection

You're never too young, or too old, to learn how money really works. The best money lessons don't always come from textbooks or school. They come from real-life experience and moments that stick.

If you have kids, involve them. Show them, don't just tell them. If you don't, reflect on how you might've learned things earlier if someone had shown you the game.

Your Takeaway

Think about your habits. How much are you spending on things you'll forget about in a few months?

What if you "hid" that money from yourself, then looked back a year later?

Try your own version of the Ziplock Bank.

Track your spending.

Set savings challenges.

Offer yourself "interest" or invest that saved money in something that builds real value.

_____

_____

_____

_____

_____

Real-Life Lessons from a Ziplock Bank with Family

CHAPTER 3:
TRYNA LOOK RICH VS. GETTIN' RICH : DA BROKE FLEX TRAP

"Floss your teeth, not your character." —
Marlo Da Motivator

Real Talk First

Some of us weren't taught how to manage money, we were taught how to flex. We wanted to look like we had it before we ever did.

Spending rent money on Jordans, putting rims on a car that barely runs, paying $1,200 a month for a car note and $600 for insurance just to impress strangers.

We thought we had to show off to feel valuable.

But here's the truth: trying to look rich keeps you broke.

It's a trap, and too many fall in it.

Real wealth doesn't need a spotlight. It walks in quiet, confident, and focused on the long game.

Money Move: Real Chain, Real Consequences

A family member of mine loves to look nice. He wears fly outfits, keeps his shoes clean, and had recently bought a flashy diamond chain, real, heavy, and expensive. When I asked why, he said it's because he should be able to, because he works hard, and because he likes nice things. Fair enough. But I warned him about wearing that kind of shine in certain hoods. His girlfriend warned him too, so much that it started causing arguments.

One day, while standing outside a gas station in the same area we grew up in, right next to his big-body Maybach, some dudes pulled up. One had a handgun, and another had a big assault-style weapon. They jumped out fast and tried to rob him.

He ran.

They chased.

He barely made it inside the gas station. There was a scuffle, caught on camera, right there at the entrance. Once they got close, he stopped fighting. They took his chain, his wallet, grabbed his phone, but tossed the phone back, probably worried about being tracked.

He made it out alive. But it could've gone a whole different way. Right there in a city he knows. In a neighborhood he's familiar with. On camera.

Truth is, he still wears big chains. Still loves the look. But the question isn't whether *he* learned anything.

The question is: **Are *you* gonna learn from his story?**

You remember that old commercial?

"You can learn a lot from a dummy."

Buckle up.

I'm not calling my family member a dummy, what I am saying is fact. You can learn a lot from dummies.

The Trap of the Broke Flex

Men especially fall into this trying to impress women or compete with others.

We drop thousands on designer belts, diamond chains, or loud outfits, all to prove something to people who don't even matter in the end.

You think the jewelry makes you look like a boss, but real bosses know the difference between assets and distractions. And here's the kicker: the flash doesn't just attract compliments. It attracts danger.

Cats out here are hungry, watching, waiting for someone to flash the wrong thing at the wrong time. Real or fake, your chain might still get snatched. And some of these folks don't just take your chain… they'll take your life with it. I've seen it happen. Over a look. Over a lie. Over a flex.

What You Can Do Instead

- You wanna wear jewelry? Get the fake stuff if you must. That way, (not if it gets taken), but when it gets taken, at least you didn't lose thousands.

- Better yet, don't wear it at all. The goal is to protect your life, not impress people.

- Buy a modest car like a Toyota or Honda. Reliable, affordable, and won't make you a target.

- Skip the $3,500 apartment to look successful.

- Buy you a used car at auction like I did.

- I once got two for $6,000 and had no car note, that's how I saved money.

• When you walk in a room, let your character speak, not your chain.

That's what real confidence looks like. That's safety. That's smart.

Money Move

Most people won't know what I have when I walk in a room. And that's on purpose.

I've built what I've built without needing to show off, and that keeps me and my family safe.

I teach my kids and anyone who listens: your confidence shouldn't depend on expensive clothes or flashy jewelry.

Wealth is quiet. It's strategic. It's smart.

Let people wonder how you did it, don't hand it to them with a loud outfit and a target on your back.

When you stop tryna look rich and start playing to win, that's when the real money moves begin.

Take Action

- Check your monthly spending, what's flex and what's foundational?

- Ask yourself who you're trying to impress, and is it worth the cost?

- Try a 30-day "no flex" challenge, no flashy purchases, just smart ones.

- Read up on quiet millionaires and how they move, then follow that example.

- Remember: the richest folks don't usually look it. And they're okay with that.

Tryna Look Rich vs. Gettin' Rich : Da Broke Flex Trap

CHAPTER 4:
REAL TALK ABOUT UNIONS THAT PAY

"A union job didn't just change my income; it changed my life."
– Kamarlo "Marlo Da Motivator" Spooner

The Power of Union Work

Let's be real. Everybody talks about getting money, but not enough people talk about how to get money with stability, benefits, and long-term growth. That's what union jobs bring to the table.

Union jobs offer:

- Better pay
- Strong benefits for you and your family
- Job protections
- A clear path to retirement through pensions

Some of the highest-paid blue-collar workers in America are union members. Sanitation workers. Truck drivers. Carpenters. Warehouse workers. Mechanics. You name it. They put in the work and their unions make sure they get their worth.

My Story: From Struggling to Secure

When I first came home from prison, I was just looking for any kind of honest work. I found a non-union carpentry job and I was grateful. The owner of the company, Top of the Line Builders, gave me my first shot. Matt, if you're reading this, thank you. That job helped me feed my family and stay focused.

I was earning about eleven or twelve dollars an hour. It wasn't a lot, but it was legal, and it was mine.

About six months later, I got into the Teamsters Union. That's when everything shifted.

My pay jumped to twenty-two dollars an hour. I had full health benefits for my wife and kids. That was huge. A few years later, I got hired by a different company, still under the Teamsters, and my pay jumped again, this time to over thirty-three dollars an hour.

Fast forward to now. Sanitation workers within Teamsters Local 70 are earning over $185,000 a year. That's before benefits. Once you add in health, welfare, and pension, their total package is worth over $225,000 a year.

That's not just a job. That's a career.

Big shout out to Teamsters Union Local 70. You changed the game for me and for so many others.

**Unions Worth Checking Out:

- **Teamsters Union (International Brotherhood of Teamsters):** One of the most powerful unions, especially strong in trucking, sanitation, warehouse, and freight.

- **IBEW (International Brotherhood of Electrical Workers):** Great for those entering electrical trades.

- **UA (United Association of Plumbers and Pipefitters):** Solid benefits, hands-on training, and high pay in the plumbing and pipefitting industry.

- **LIUNA (Laborers' International Union of North America):** For general laborers and construction workers with opportunities for training and certification.

- **Ironworkers Union:** For those working in structural steel, bridges, and major construction projects.

No matter your background or where you're starting from, a union can help you level up your income, protect your rights, and provide security for your family. Just like it did for me.

Keep building. Keep rising. Keep Focus. Keep Winning

_____

_____

_____

_____

_____

_____

_____

_____

Looka here mane!

You've read and studied da blueprint.

You've seen da mindset, da hustle, da comeback, and da strategy.

Now it's time to stop playing small.

Time to stop sitting on the sidelines.

Time to stop making other people rich while staying stuck yourself.

You got da game now.

And as people used to say, game recognizes game.

Keep building.

Keep stacking.

Keep passing it on.

I'll see you at da top.

But if you don't put in that work and grind hard for it…

I guess you just have to look up, and you'll see ya guy!!!

Because I ain't playin.
Remember – Winners Win and Loser, Well they Lose

Kamarlo Spooner
"Marlo Da Motivator"

WINNERS WIN AND LOSERS. WELL, THEY JUST LOSE!

Last time that I checked. You were a winner!! Remember:
It's Not Impossible,
It's I'm Possible
Because You Are!!!!

Da Money Manual

www.ingramcontent.com/pod-product-compliance
Lightning Source LLC
Chambersburg PA
CBHW061730070526
44583CB00024B/3078